Photo by Michal Daniel

Jessica Hecht, Kevin Carroll, and Sandra Oh in a scene from the New York Shakespeare Festival production of *Stop Kiss*.

STOP KISS

BY
DIANA SON

★

★

DRAMATISTS
PLAY SERVICE
INC.

for Jessica, Sandra, Kevin, Rick, Saul, Saundra,
Brooke, C.J., Buzz and Jo

STOP KISS was produced by the New York Shakespeare Festival (George C. Wolfe, Producer; Rosemarie Tichler, Artistic Producer; Mark Litvin, Managing Director) in New York City on December 6, 1998. It was directed by Jo Bonney; the set design was by Narelle Sissons; the lighting design was by James Vermeulen; the sound design was by David Van Tieghem; the costume design was by Kaye Voyce; the production dramaturg was Mervin P. Antonio; and the production stage manager was Buzz Cohen. The cast was as follows:

CALLIE	Jessica Hecht
SARA	Sandra Oh
GEORGE	Kevin Carroll
PETER	Rick Holmes
MRS. WINSLEY/NURSE	Saundra McClain
DETECTIVE COLE	Saul Stein

CAST

Callie — late 20s to early 30s.
Sara — mid-20s to early 30s.
George — late 20s to early 30s.
Peter — mid-20s to early 30s.
Mrs. Winsley — early 40s to early 50s.
Detective Cole — late 30s to mid-40s.
Nurse — late 30s to mid-40s. Can be doubled with Mrs. Winsley.

SETTING

New York City.

TIME

Now.

Note: The cast should reflect
the ethnic diversity of New York City.

Stop Kiss is an intermissionless play.
It should be performed without interruption.

STOP KISS

SCENE ONE

Callie's apartment. Callie puts on a CD. Something '70s and great to dance to like The Emotions' "Best of My Love." She ceremoniously closes all the blinds in her apartment, making sure each blade is turned over. She locks the front door and puts a piece of black tape over the peephole. As the vocals begin, Callie lip-syncs to the song with the polish of someone who has their own private karaoke often. The phone rings. Callie turns off the CD like a busted teenager and picks up the phone.*

CALLIE. Hi George ... yeah I know I'm late, I forgot this person is coming to my house at — *(Callie checks her watch.)* — shit! ... Well I would bring her along but I don't even know her. She's some friend of an old friend of someone I used to be frie — she just moved to New York and I said that I'd — I can't, what if she's some big dud and we all have a miserable time ... Exactly, you'll all blame me. Give me half an hour, tops. *(She sets the phone down. Her buzzer buzzes.)* Yes?

SARA. *(Offstage. Tentative.)* It's Sara and —

CALLIE. Come on up! *(Callie buzzes her in and looks at all the junk on her sofa: newspapers, several pairs of dirty socks, a box of Kleenex, mail, a couple videotapes, and a bra. She picks up the bra and heads for the bedroom. The doorbell rings. Callie hides the bra and opens the door. Sara is holding a pet carrier.)* Hi.

SARA. You're Callie.

CALLIE. Yes.

SARA. I'm Sara — *(She looks at the pet carrier.)* This is Caesar and

*See Special Note on Songs and Recordings on copyright page.

7

I can't believe you're doing this. *(Callie gestures at the couch.)*

CALLIE. Come in. Please uh sit —

SARA. Some apartment.

CALLIE. I was cleaning.

SARA. It's huge — and the neighborhood — *(Sara sits on a pile of books.)*

CALLIE. You can't be comfortable.

SARA. Oh I am.

CALLIE. Are you sure?

SARA. Very.

CALLIE. — Just ... let me get rid of this stuff. *(Callie gathers an armful of junk and heads towards her bedroom. As soon as she turns her back, Sara sits up and pulls out a large key ring full of sharp pointy keys and a candlestick from under her as she silently mouths "ow." She moves the objects to another part of the sofa, covers them with leftover junk — pulling out the keys so that they show — and makes a space for Callie. Callie reenters.)* Coffee!

SARA. — would be great. Listen, this is so nice of you —

CALLIE. I was thinking about getting a cat anyway. Oh, my keys! This'll give me a chance to see if I can hack it.

SARA. That's how I feel about New York.

CALLIE. *(Sounds familiar.)* Oh yes. *(Sara hops up and follows Callie who heads towards the kitchen.)*

SARA. How long have you been here?

CALLIE. Eleven years.

SARA. I've lived in St. Louis my whole life. My parents live like, half an hour away. I go there for dinner when it's not even anybody's birthday. Things there — it's been, it *is* so —

CALLIE. Easy?

SARA. So easy.

CALLIE. It's hard here.

SARA. Good — *great*, I can't wait.

CALLIE. Yeah, you uh — what do you ... do?

SARA. I teach. Third grade.

CALLIE. Well it won't be hard finding a job.

SARA. I already have one.

CALLIE. Where?

SARA. P.S. 32 in the Bronx.

CALLIE. What was the school like that you came from?

SARA. Society of Friends, a Quaker school. *(Callie bursts into laughter.)*

CALLIE. I'm not — I'm not laughing *at* you, I'm laughing … *around* —

SARA. It's obviously — it's *very* … but I can do good work there.

CALLIE. I'm sure you're a good teacher.

SARA. No you don't know, but I am. *(Pause.)*

CALLIE. Where in the Bronx?

SARA. Tremont.

CALLIE. Is that where … Taft, is it Taft?

SARA. Taft High School?

CALLIE. You've heard of it?

SARA. Mm-hm.

CALLIE. You know there was a guy who taught there, this rich white guy —

SARA. Yes I know. *(Pause.)*

CALLIE. He got killed —

SARA. By a student. I'm here on a fellowship set up in his name.

CALLIE. How long is the fellowship?

SARA. Two years. *(Callie reenters, offers Sara a coffee mug and raises hers in a toast.)*

CALLIE. Well, congratulations —

SARA. Thank you.

CALLIE. *Best* of luck –– *(Sara nods.)* And … if it gets too rough — go home. *(Callie touches her mug to Sara's but Sara doesn't reciprocate.)*

SARA. What brought *you* to New York? *(Callie inhales to prepare for her long and interesting answer, then realizes she has none.)*

CALLIE. College.

SARA. And what keeps you?

CALLIE. Keeps me from what?

SARA. What do you *do?*

CALLIE. I … ruin things for everyone else.

SARA. You're Rudolph Giuliani?

CALLIE. I'm a traffic reporter for a 24-hour news radio station.

SARA. *(Impressed.)* Helicopters!

CALLIE. "The inbound lane at the Holland Tunnel is closed due to a car accident. The Brooklyn-bound lane of the Williamsburg

9

Bridge is under construction through 2002. The D train is not running due to a track fire. You can't get in. You can't get out. You can't get around. I'll be back in 10 minutes to tell you that nothing has changed."

SARA. Does that get to you? *(Callie shrugs.)*

CALLIE. It's a living. *(Sara checks out the apartment.)*

SARA. How long have you lived in this apartment?

CALLIE. Five years — well, two by myself — it's a funny — not ha-ha — story.

SARA. It's OK. *(i.e., you don't have to tell me.)*

CALLIE. I moved in here with my boyfriend Tom. This was his aunt's apartment, she lived here for 20 years.

SARA. Your rent must be —

CALLIE. Lucky.

SARA. *You* are.

CALLIE. Well, I got the apartment, he got ... my sister.

SARA. Oh.

CALLIE. They live in L.A. now. It's perfect.

SARA. Well at least, I don't mean to be crass but —

CALLIE. Yes, no, well I ... like the apartment.

SARA. It's as big as mine and I'm sharing it with two other people.

CALLIE. Are they — did you ... move here with any of them?

SARA. No, they came with the apartment. They're a couple. It's kind of awkward, but, he's sweet, she's sweet, they seem to have a —

CALLIE. — sweet?

SARA. — relationshipthey'refine.

CALLIE. *(Nods.)* It's awkward.

SARA. Rents are *so* — everything is —

CALLIE. It's impossible to live here. *(Pause. Sara studies Callie.)*

SARA. *You love it.*

CALLIE. You know, Sara, I've actually been to St. Louis and it's a quaint, pretty city but — what's the point of that? Everyone's still got their cars all geared up with clubs and car alarms and computerized keys. And you have to drive all the way across town to get to the good cheap places to eat. And *drive*, I mean you're in a city and you have to *drive* to get around?

SARA. Where did you grow up?

CALLIE. Tiny town upstate.

SARA. Industrial?

CALLIE. Countrified suburb. Tractor display in the middle of the mall.

SARA. Pretty, though?

CALLIE. I can't connect with mountains, trees, the little animals — they snub me. You know how you can be with two other people and you're all having a great time. Then the person sitting next to you says something in French and the two of them burst into laughter, best laugh anyone's had all night. And you're left out because you took Spanish in the seventh grade, not French. That's what nature does to me. Speaks French to the other people at the table. *(Slight pause.)*

SARA. I hate jazz.

CALLIE. *You do?*

SARA. I don't usually say that out loud because then people think I don't have a soul or something but I don't like the way it sounds. I don't like saxophones.

CALLIE. My sister played the saxophone.

SARA. I'm sorry —

CALLIE. I hate my sister.

SARA. The one who —

CALLIE. Yeah!

SARA. I hate your sister too. *(Callie gives up a surprised smile; Sara does too. They hold it just a beat longer than normal, then Sara looks away.)*

CALLIE. So — do your friends think you're crazy?

SARA. Pff. Forget it. And my *parents* and Peter?

CALLIE. Huh?

SARA. — my ex. I mean I've never lived away from them. Even when I was in college I came home every weekend.

CALLIE. Close family.

SARA. It's ... a cult. It's embarrassing, I should've moved ... I mean, you were what, eighteen?

CALLIE. Don't look at me. I was going to go to one of those colleges that advertise on matchbook covers. My guidance counselor filled out my application to NYU.

SARA. I had to interview five times to get this fellowship. By the fourth one I had a rabbit's foot, rosary beads, crystals, a tiger's tooth, and a Polynesian *tiki* all in my purse — now that

11

I got this fellowship I have every god to pay. *(Callie hands Sara a Magic Eight-Ball.)* What should I ask it?

CALLIE. Something whose answer you won't take too seriously.

SARA. *(Addressing the ball.)* Was moving to New York a good idea? *(She shakes the ball, then looks at it.)* It's sort of in between two of them.

CALLIE. That means yes. *(Another shared smile. Sara stands up.)*

SARA. I should go, I'm taking up too much of your — *(Callie looks at her watch.)*

CALLIE. I told some friends I would meet them, otherwise I wish —

SARA. You should've said —

CALLIE. No — no —

SARA. I didn't mean to keep —

CALLIE. What're you doing this weekend?

SARA. I don't know. Unpacking. But then I gotta do something New Yorky, don't I?

CALLIE. Do you want to come over and I'll take you around the neighborhood? Show you some fun places to go to and eat —

SARA. Yes!

CALLIE. And you can hang out here, spend some time with ... is it Caesar? *(Sara rushes to the pet carrier.)*

SARA. Caesar, forgive me. He hates being in this thing.

CALLIE. Let him out. *(Sara does.)*

SARA. He may be a little shy at first, in a new place with a new person —

CALLIE. You could come and visit him. Just let me know. I hope you'll feel —

SARA. Thanks, Callie.

CALLIE. For nothing, for what.

SCENE TWO

A hospital examination room. Callie is sitting on an exam table buttoning the top button of her shirt. Detective Cole stands in front of her.

DET. COLE. Was he coming on to you, trying to pick you up?

CALLIE. He was just saying stuff, guy stuff, stupid kind of —

DET. COLE. What did you do? *(She folds her arms protectively across her stomach like it's tender.)*

CALLIE. I — I wanted to leave —

DET. COLE. Your girlfriend?

CALLIE. My friend — Sara ... said ... something —

DET. COLE. What.

CALLIE. "Leave us alone" or something.

DET. COLE. And that's what set him off?

CALLIE. N — n — yeah. Well, she said — but then he said something back and she told him ... she said something — upset him.

DET. COLE. What'd she say?

CALLIE. ... She sai — I think —

DET. COLE. What.

CALLIE. She told him to fuck off. Then he hit her.

DET. COLE. He hit her with his fist?

CALLIE. He hit her in her back then he grabbed her away —

DET. COLE. Grabbed her from you?

CALLIE. I — I was holding on to her arm with my hand like this — *(She puts her hand on her other elbow.)* I wanted us to leave. But then he grabbed her and started banging her head against the building. And then he smashed her head against his knee — like one of those wrestlers — that's when she lost consciousness — and then he smashed her again. *(Callie refolds her arms across her stomach. Det. Cole looks at his report.)*

DET. COLE. This was at Bleecker and West 11th — that little park.

13

CALLIE. Yes.

DET. COLE. At 4:15 in the morning?

CALLIE. Yes.

DET. COLE. What were you doing there? *(Callie shakes her head.)*

CALLIE. ... Just ... walking around.

DET. COLE. Which bar were you at?

CALLIE. Excuse me?

DET. COLE. 4:15, honey, that's closing time.

CALLIE. Well we had been ... we were at the White Horse Tavern.

DET. COLE. The White Horse. On Hudson Street.

CALLIE. Yes.

DET. COLE. Was there a good crowd there?

CALLIE. ... Yeah? Pretty crowded.

DET. COLE. Did anyone at the White Horse try to pick you up, buy you or your friend a drink?

CALLIE. No.

DET. COLE. Did you talk to anyone?

CALLIE. Just to each other mostly.

DET. COLE. What did the bartender look like?

CALLIE. Excuse me?

DET. COLE. Bartender.

CALLIE. ... It was a man.

DET. COLE. Short, stocky guy? Salt-and-pepper hair?

CALLIE. No.

DET. COLE. Kind of tall, skinny guy with a receding hairline? I know a couple of guys there.

CALLIE. I didn't really get a good look at him — Sara ordered the drinks. But I think he was tall.

DET. COLE. I'll go talk to him. Could be someone followed you from the bar. Maybe there was someone suspicious-acting that you didn't notice. Bartender mighta seen something you didn't or talked to someone. What'd the bad guy look like?

CALLIE. He was tall.

DET. COLE. Like the bartender.

CALLIE. He was big — sort of, like he worked out.

DET. COLE. Was he black?

CALLIE. No.

DET. COLE. Hispanic?

14

CALLIE. It was dark, I couldn't —

DET. COLE. Short hair, long hair —

CALLIE. Short. Wavy, dark brown.

DET. COLE. You remember what he was wearing?

CALLIE. He had a leather jacket ... jeans ... some kind of boots. He was twenty — something, maybe mid.

DET. COLE. Like a college kid? Frat boy?

CALLIE. No.

DET. COLE. Like a punk?

CALLIE. No.

DET. COLE. Like what then?

CALLIE. ... I don't know.

DET. COLE. Any markings on the jacket? A name or symbol?

CALLIE. No.

DET. COLE. So he sees a couple of good-looking girls walking — were you drunk?

CALLIE. Not at all.

DET. COLE. — he gives 'em a line, one of the women tells him to fuck off and he beats her into a coma. Anything else you want to tell me?

CALLIE. That's — that's what I ... remember.

DET. COLE. Doctor done with you?

CALLIE. I think.

DET. COLE. All right, I need you to go somewhere with me right now and look at some pictures.

CALLIE. Can you bring them here?

DET. COLE. I need to take you there.

CALLIE. Because, my friend — if my friend —

DET. COLE. They say she's out of the woods in terms of life or —

CALLIE. But if she wakes up —

SCENE THREE

Callie's apartment. Callie hangs up her and Sara's jackets.
Sara sits on the couch, which is now clean.

SARA. I mean that's the way I am with the kids.

CALLIE. Sure, with kids it's OK.

SARA. Why just them? Listen, every day when I walk by this park this guy, he's all cracked out, says something to me, you know, something nasty and I just lower my head and walk by.

CALLIE. Yep.

SARA. But yesterday, one of my students, Malik, is waiting for me outside the school and says he wants to walk me to the subway. So I say "sure," thinking maybe he has a problem he wants to tell me about. So, we're walking and we pass by the park and I'm worried. "Is this crackhead gonna mention my vagina in front of this eight-year-old boy?" Sure enough, it's "pussy this" and "booty that" and Malik says, "This is my teacher, watch your mouth." And the guy shuts up.

CALLIE. Still —

SARA. Freaking eight-year-old boy. I should be able to do that for myself.

CALLIE. The best thing to do is walk on by.

SARA. But it worked. *(The phone rings. Sara looks up but Callie doesn't.)*

CALLIE. Next time, just walk on by.

SARA. Why, what's ever happened to you?

CALLIE. Nothing and that's why. *(The machine clicks on.)*

GEORGE'S VOICE ON MACHINE. Hey Callie, it's George. Where are you? *(Callie starts to pick up the phone, then stops.)* Jasmine and Lidia and I are at the Sinatra bar. We'll be here for a while so come hang out. Bye. *(The machine clicks off.)*

SARA. I should go.

16

CALLIE. No no, they'll be there for hours.

SARA. I've taken up your whole —

CALLIE. Are you hungry? We could order in something. There's Polish, Indian, Cuban, there's a pretty good Vietnamese —

SARA. Are you sure you don't — I've never had Vietnamese —

CALLIE. I'll show you the menu. *(Callie hops up and goes into the kitchen.)* Something to drink? Beer?

SARA. Yes to beer. *(Sara leans her head towards the phone.)* Were those friends from work?

CALLIE. Oh no, the people at my job are a bunch of stiffs — can you imagine? They listen to the same news reports every ten minutes for eight hours a day. They repeat themselves even in regular conversations. No, George — the guy on the phone — Lidia, Jasmine ... Rico, Sally, Ben — we were all friends in college and now we're stuck to each other. I think we're someone's science experiment, we just don't know it. A study in overdependency.

SARA. Is George your boyfriend? *(Callie returns, carrying two beers. She hands a beer and menu to Sara.)*

CALLIE. I like the noodle dishes, they're on the back. *(Sara takes the menu.)* George and I ... are friends. Who sleep together. But date other people. Sometimes for long periods of time. We've been doing this since we were ... 20. Although he *never* likes anyone I'm dating, he's unabashedly — and I admit I can get jealous when he's — but at least I try to hide it, I'm pretty good at it too. It's only *after* they've broken up that I — Anyway, we'll probably get married. *(Sara gets the Eight-Ball and shakes it. She looks up at Callie.)* Or not.

SARA. It's stuck between two again.

CALLIE. Why's that keep happening to you?

SARA. Me? I think you have it rigged. *(Callie takes the ball and shakes it. She looks at its answer: It's between two. Sara tries to look — .)*

CALLIE. OK, OK.

SARA. All my friends are married or getting engaged, having babies or wishing they were — and lately when I hear about it, I think — why?

CALLIE. Why not?

SARA. Marriage. Why would you say to anyone, "I will stay with you even if I outgrow you." *(Pause.)*

17

CALLIE. *(Remembering.)* Peter. *(Sara is unresponsive, then finally nods.)* Did you leave him to come here?
SARA. ... No.
CALLIE. Mm ... C-minus.
SARA. In what.
CALLIE. Acting. *(Sara looks down.)* I'm sorry —
SARA. No no —
CALLIE. I'm prying —
SARA. No, that's not why —
CALLIE. I hope I didn't —
SARA. No, it's OK. *(Slight pause.)*
CALLIE. Did you decide what you wanted to order?
SARA. I moved out from our apartment — we lived together — and moved in with my parents about a month ago. I came here from there.
CALLIE. How — how long —
SARA. Seven years.
CALLIE. *Seven* ... so you must still be —
SARA. — Finally. Finally where I want to be. I'll stay in New York for two years and then I'm going to take off.
CALLIE. Let me guess: India.
SARA. A for effort, but no. Australia, Malaysia, Indonesia, Micronesia —
CALLIE. All the countries that sound like skin rashes?
SARA. Peter said, "What about Anesthesia?" Speaking — what time is it?
CALLIE. Almost 6:00.
SARA. Hm.
CALLIE. What?
SARA. Oh, he left a message on my machine saying he was going to call at 6:00. He wants to come visit. He manages a restaurant in St. Louis so he wants to come and check out some of the special places here.
CALLIE. You'd better hurry.
SARA. I couldn't make it in 15 minutes.
CALLIE. You could if you took a cab. *(Slight pause.)*
SARA. But then I wouldn't have Vietnamese food.
CALLIE. We could do it another time.

SARA. I just started this beer. *(Pause.)*
CALLIE. You wouldn't want to waste a beer.
SARA. That's what I was thinking.
CALLIE. Cheers. *(They tap glasses. There is a sudden loud and rhythmic clomping on the ceiling. Callie doesn't respond.)* I always get this. It's not too spicy.
SARA. What is that?
CALLIE. Crispy squid in a little salt and —
SARA. No, what is *that?*
CALLIE. Huh? Oh. Every Thursday and Saturday at 6.
SARA. What.
CALLIE. I think he teaches horses how to river dance.
SARA. Have you complained?
CALLIE. It happens at exactly the same time twice a week for an hour. I just make sure I'm out or doing something loud.
SARA. Let's go up there.
CALLIE. No no —
SARA. Why not?
CALLIE. We gotta stay here and wait for the food.
SARA. We haven't ordered it yet.
CALLIE. *(About the food.)* Yeah so what do you want.
SARA. Chicken.
CALLIE. What kind of chicken?
SARA. You're chicken.
CALLIE. No I'm not, I'm smart.
SARA. All right, I'll go.
CALLIE. Sara. Come on, don't. Please. *(Slight pause.)*
SARA. OK.
CALLIE. I'm gonna order. What do you want?
SARA. Aw, come on, let's go!

SCENE FOUR

Police station house. Mrs. Winsley sits behind a table that Det.
Cole is sitting on. She's wearing a sharply tailored business suit.

MRS. WINSLEY. He called them pussy-eating dykes.
DET. COLE. Come on, why would he call them that?
MRS. WINSLEY. Two women in a West Village park at 4:00 in the morning? What's the chance they're *not* dykes.
DET. COLE. You tell me. You live in the West Village.
MRS. WINSLEY. My husband and I have lived there for eight years.
DET. COLE. Like the neighborhood?
MRS. WINSLEY. I sure do.
DET. COLE. Lot of clubs and bars there.
MRS. WINSLEY. They even have ones for straight people.
DET. COLE. Is that why you live there?
MRS. WINSLEY. My husband and I have a beautiful apartment, Detective Cole. In a safe building on an otherwise quiet street. The fact that it's Graceland for gay people doesn't matter to me.
DET. COLE. So what were these girls doing?
MRS. WINSLEY. I didn't see —
DET. COLE. Were they making out, rubbing up against each other —
MRS. WINSLEY. I didn't see anything till I heard the other one screaming. I went to the window, then I called 911.
DET. COLE. What'd you see then?
MRS. WINSLEY. He was beating on the both of them. I yelled down that I called the cops and I threw a couple flowerpots at him. My spider plants —
DET. COLE. So the screams woke you up?
MRS. WINSLEY. I was in bed but up. Reading.
DET. COLE. 4:30 in the morning?
MRS. WINSLEY. I'm a fitful sleeper.
DET. COLE. You ever take anything?

20

MRS. WINSLEY. No.

DET. COLE. So you weren't groggy or half-asleep?

MRS. WINSLEY. No.

DET. COLE. And you're sure you heard him call them dykes.

MRS. WINSLEY. I'm sure.

DET. COLE. And your husband? *(No response.)* Your husband?

MRS. WINSLEY. He missed all the excitement.

DET. COLE. What'd he — sleep right through it? *(Mrs. Winsley avoids his eyes.)* Oh ... he wasn't home. 4:30 in the — is he a doctor?

MRS. WINSLEY. No.

DET. COLE. ... Investment banker?

MRS. WINSLEY. Ha!

DET. COLE. Fire chief?

MRS. WINSLEY. He's a book editor, Detective Cole.

DET. COLE. I didn't know book editors worked so late.

MRS. WINSLEY. They don't.

DET. COLE. Was he ... out having drinks with some buddies?

MRS. WINSLEY. He was obviously out, wasn't he.

DET. COLE. So you were waiting up for him.

MRS. WINSLEY. I'm a fitful sleeper, Detective. Have been since before I married him and those two girls are lucky that I am and that I was up and that I did something.

DET. COLE. You called 911.

MRS. WINSLEY. And my flowerpots.

DET. COLE. Did you hit him?

MRS. WINSLEY. They fell near him. He stopped and took off.

DET. COLE. You stopped him.

MRS. WINSLEY. Well it wasn't the cops, took 30 minutes for them to show up. You'd think it was Harlem, not the West Village.

SCENE FIVE

Callie's apartment. Callie walks on wearing jeans and carrying a fresh bouquet of flowers. She places them in a vase. She goes into her bedroom and reenters with several hangers of clothes. She looks at herself in the mirror as she holds up a tube top in front of her — too slutty — then drops the top onto the floor. She picks up a shirt and holds it up in front of her — too butch — then throws it onto the floor. She tries on a short skirt but it won't get past her hips. She looks around — as if she were in a public dressing room — then puts her jeans back on. She puts on a third top — it looks like something Sara would wear. The front door buzzer buzzes. Callie buzzes without asking who it is. She goes to take the flowers out of the vase but accidentally knocks the whole thing over. She gets that damn skirt and uses it to wipe up the mess. There is a knock on the door. Callie gets to the door just in time to open it. George walks in and stops in the puddle.

GEORGE. Hey Cal, when did they paint the — whoops! *(Callie is stunned to see George but plays it off like it's about the puddle.)*
CALLIE. George! *(George looks down.)*
GEORGE. Did you get a puppy?
CALLIE. Yeah, right. *(Callie stands up. They kiss lightly on the lips.)*
GEORGE. So you're all right, huh?
CALLIE. Yeah, what?
GEORGE. No, I haven't heard from you in a while.
CALLIE. I'm fine, I'm fine ... busy. *(Callie goes to the kitchen to throw away the skirt. George takes off his jacket.)*
GEORGE. Lidia said she called you about that book you were looking for, you didn't call her back.
CALLIE. ... I forgot.
GEORGE. She got that job, you know.
CALLIE. No, I didn't! *(George stretches himself out on the couch,*

stacking a pile of pillows behind his head.)
GEORGE. Yeah, she's really excited. *(Callie looks disapprovingly at his move.)* We're gonna take her out on Friday night so try not to be fine but busy that night, OK? *(He grabs the remote and clicks the TV on.)*
CALLIE. I'll remember. Um, George — *(He looks at his watch.)*
GEORGE. I know, I know, we can watch your show, I just want to check to see what the score is.
CALLIE. I have plans for tonight.
GEORGE. Oh yeah, what?
CALLIE. I'm meeting someone for dinner. *(George turns off the TV and sits up.)*
GEORGE. You have a date?
CALLIE. No!
GEORGE. With *who?*
CALLIE. It's not a date, I'm just meeting my friend Sara for dinner.
GEORGE. Who the hell is Sara?
CALLIE. I told you, that friend of a friend of a — *(Refreshing his memory.)* She's new in town, I'm taking care of her cat —
GEORGE. I thought you said she was a big loser.
CALLIE. I said I didn't know, but now I do — she's not.
GEORGE. So what is she?
CALLIE. What.
GEORGE. What's she do?
CALLIE. She teaches up in the Bronx.
GEORGE. Oh, so she's a nut.
CALLIE. There's something wrong with us.
GEORGE. Why?
CALLIE. Because that's what I thought when she told me.
GEORGE. You have to wonder about people who want to do stuff like that. What does she want to do — save a life? Give a kid a chance? Or just feel good about trying.
CALLIE. She won a fellowship. She *competed* to get this job.
GEORGE. To teach in the Bronx? What'd the losers get? *(The front door buzzer buzzes. Callie buzzes back.)* You don't ask who it is anymore?
CALLIE. It's her.
GEORGE. You thought it was her when you buzzed me in.

CALLIE. You're right, that was a mistake. *(Sara knocks at the door. Callie holds George's jacket open for him.)* OK. Please leave now.

GEORGE. Why?

CALLIE. Because I gotta go. *(He stands up.)*

GEORGE. I'll walk out with you.

CALLIE. But I'm not leaving yet.

GEORGE. Huh? *(Callie opens the door and Sara walks in.)*

CALLIE. Hey.

SARA. Hi, here, these are ... *(Sara shyly hands Callie a small bouquet of baby roses. Callie takes them.)*

CALLIE. Thank you. They're so —

SARA. They're — babies. *(Callie and Sara take turns trying to kiss each other on the cheek and missing. Finally Callie turns away, takes the other flowers out of the vase and puts the roses in.)*

CALLIE. I was just going to throw these out. *(She crosses to the kitchen.)*

SARA. Hey, did you see they're filming a movie or something on the next block? Do you think we could stop on our way to the restaurant and watch for a while? *(George steps out.)*

GEORGE. It's *NYPD Bl* — *(Sara starts.)* Oop — didn't mean to scare you.

SARA. No no, you didn't. *(He crosses to her and extends his hand.)*

GEORGE. I'm George. *(Sara shakes his hand.)*

SARA. Oh, *George*, I've heard so much about you!

GEORGE. *(Can't say the same thing.)* ... Nice to meet you. *(Callie comes out of the kitchen.)*

CALLIE. Oh, sorry. Sara, this is George. George, this is —

GEORGE. We did this.

CALLIE. Good. *(To Sara.)* We should go.

GEORGE. Where're you guys having dinner?

CALLIE. *(Tries to slip it past him.)* Vong. *(George looks at Callie.)*

GEORGE. Dressed like that?

CALLIE. I didn't have time —

SARA. *(Consoling.)* You look great.

GEORGE. Well, tell me what you get.

SARA. Have you ever been?

GEORGE. Out of my league.

SARA. *(To Callie.)* Is it expensive? I don't want you to —

24

CALLIE. It's not expensive.

GEORGE. *(To Callie.)* You're treating? Then I wanna —

CALLIE. *(To George.)* You still owe me for my birthday.

SARA. Let's go dutch, Callie.

CALLIE. It's my treat.

GEORGE. What's the occasion? *(Silence. There is none.)*

SARA. Actually, we're celebrating the fact that today LaChandra, one of my students, wrote her name for the very first time. *(Callie looks down at herself.)*

CALLIE. I'm changing. *(She runs off.)*

GEORGE. That's right, you're a teacher.

SARA. Mm-hm.

GEORGE. Kindergarten?

SARA. Third grade.

GEORGE. And this kid wrote her name for the first time?

SARA. Perfectly.

GEORGE. Isn't that —

SARA. Wonderful?

GEORGE. *(Won over.)* ... Yeah, isn't it? *(Callie reenters wearing the blouse she started off wearing.)*

CALLIE. *(To Sara.)* We should go, our reservation's at 8:00.

SARA. Do we have time to stop by? The *NYPD Blue* —

CALLIE. Sure. *(Sara starts for the door.)*

GEORGE. OK, well um, bye. Nice to meet you.

SARA. Don't you want to come with us and watch them filming? *(George flashes Callie a furtive look.)*

GEORGE. Mmm, I think I'll wait until it's on TV. *(He looks at Callie; she ushers him out the door.)*

CALLIE. Meanie.

GEORGE. Never take *me* to Vong. *(Callie closes the door and locks it.)*

SCENE SIX

Police station house. Callie sits in an interview room.
Detective Cole enters.

DET. COLE. Hey, thanks for coming in. You want some coffee?
CALLIE. Thank you, I'm fine. *(He flips through his report.)*
DET. COLE. We were talking about the White Horse Tavern last time, right? On Hudson Street?
CALLIE. Yes.
DET. COLE. That's a famous bar, you know? Has a long literary tradition. They say Dylan Thomas died waiting for a drink there.
CALLIE. ... I hadn't heard.
DET. COLE. I talked to the bartender there. I told you I wanted to ask him if he noticed anyone suspicious there that night. Maybe someone paying attention to you and your friend that you didn't notice.
CALLIE. Yes, you said.
DET. COLE. I went in and talked to Stacy, she said she don't remember you and your friend coming in.
CALLIE. It was pretty crowded. *(Slight pause.)*
DET. COLE. Do you remember telling me that the bartender at the White Horse Tavern that night was a tall *guy?*
CALLIE. Sara ordered the drinks.
DET. COLE. So you didn't get a good look at the bartender.
CALLIE. I didn't.
DET. COLE. Not even enough to tell if it was a girl or a guy.
CALLIE. I'm sorry.
DET. COLE. So after you leave the White Horse, you and your friend go for a walk. You end up in that park area outside the playground. And you're ... doing what?
CALLIE. We were sitting on one of the benches, talking to each other ... when this guy says something.
DET. COLE. What'd he say?

26

CALLIE. Something like, "Hey, you want to party — "

DET. COLE. What did you say?

CALLIE. I didn't.

DET. COLE. Sara said something.

CALLIE. Yes.

DET. COLE. So she provoked him.

CALLIE. What!?

DET. COLE. She told him to "fuck off" and that's when he hit her, right?

CALLIE. No.

DET. COLE. I mean, if the two of you had ignored him or walked away, this wouldn't have happened, would it?

CALLIE. If *he* hadn't started —

DET. COLE. But Sara had to say something and that's what got him pissed, that's why he wanted to hit her. Why did she say something?

CALLIE. He started it, he —

DET. COLE. All right. *He* must have said something first — something that upset her. What upset her so much?

CALLIE. He was bothering —

DET. COLE. What did he say? She said "leave us alone," and then he said what? *(Callie doesn't respond.)*

DET. COLE. Did he call her something?

CALLIE. What?

DET. COLE. Like a name?

CALLIE. No.

DET. COLE. What's a name that might upset her?

CALLIE. I don't know.

DET. COLE. How about bitch?

CALLIE. No.

DET. COLE. He didn't call her a bitch?

CALLIE. I don't —

DET. COLE. A pussy-eating bitch? *(Callie looks at Det. Cole.)*

CALLIE. No.

DET. COLE. What'd he say, then —

CALLIE. He shouldn't've —

DET. COLE. What'd he call her?

CALLIE. He called —

DET. COLE. What?

CALLIE. A fucking —

DET. COLE. Say it!

CALLIE. Fucking dyke! Pussy-eating dykes — both of us.

DET. COLE. Why would he say that, why would he call you that? Two nice girls sitting on a park bench talking, why would he call you dykes. *(Pause.)*

CALLIE. Because we were kissing. *(Det. Cole gestures — there it is.)* It was the first — We didn't know he was there. Until he said something. "Hey, save some of that for me." Sara told him to leave us alone. I couldn't believe she — then he offered to pay us. He said he'd give us 50 bucks if we went to a motel with him and let him watch. He said we could dry hump or whatever we like to do — turns him on just to see it. I grabbed her arm and started walking away. He came after us, called us fucking dykes — pussy-eating dykes. Sara told him to fuck off. I couldn't believe — he came up and punched her in the back, then he grabbed her and pulled her away. I yelled for someone to call the police. He pushed her against the building and started banging her head against the building. He told her to watch her cunt-licking mouth. But he had his hand over her jaw, she couldn't — she just made these mangled — she was trying to breathe. I came up behind him and grabbed his hair — he turned around and punched me in the stomach. I threw up, it got on him. Sara tried to get away but he grabbed her and started banging her head against his knee. I tried to hold his arms back but he was stronger — he knocked her out. He pushed me to the ground and started kicking me. Someone yelled something — "cops are coming" — and he took off in the opposite direction. West. He was limping. He hurt his knee. *(She looks at Det. Cole.)* That's what happened.

SCENE SEVEN

*Callie's apartment. Sara is sprawled out on the couch hold-
ing several giant playing cards in her hand. She places a
card on the discard pile and drains a glass of wine. Callie
brings a bottle of red wine from the kitchen; an empty one
stands on the table.*

SARA. OK. If you're in someone else's bathroom and they have
the toilet paper coming out from the bottom instead of the top —
CALLIE. I hate that!
SARA. Do you change it or leave it the way it is.
CALLIE. What do you mean change it? You'd change somebody
else's toilet roll?
SARA. Yeah, if I was gonna use it a couple times.
CALLIE. Pfff.
SARA. All right, you go next.
CALLIE. So if you were driving down a highway and saw a pothole
in the road ahead, what would you do, straddle or swerve?
SARA. Mm, straddle. You?
CALLIE. Straddle.
SARA. *(About Callie.)* Swerve.
CALLIE. Nah-ah.
SARA. Yes you would.
CALLIE. *(A second scenario.)* Cat in the road.
SARA. Caesar! — say a rabbit.
CALLIE. OK, a rabbit. Straddle, swerve, or brake.
SARA. *(Like this is an option.)* Straddle a rabbit.
CALLIE. Sport Utility Vehicle — four-wheel drive, you could.
(Callie sits down, picks up her hand, and discards.)
SARA. Screech to a brake, check the rabbit, then — smoke. You?
CALLIE. Brake.
SARA. *Swerve.*
CALLIE. Why do you keep saying that?

29

SARA. This is you — *(She pretends to be Callie driving then swerving. Callie puts her cards down.)*

CALLIE. These cards are driving me nuts.

SARA. One more hand, please. *(Callie picks the cards back up.)*

CALLIE. Can I ask you something about your job?

SARA. Yep.

CALLIE. Why did you want it? *→ why are you constantly running at things that are hard?*

SARA. You mean this fellowship?

CALLIE. Public school, the Bronx — teaching.

SARA. Instead of private school, St. Louis — teaching?

CALLIE. That's what you're used to, right?

SARA. It's where I *worked* for five years, I never got used to it. I mean, I never went to private school. We all went to the cruddy public school — I mean, it was cruddy compared to the private school, it's *the Sorbonne* compared to where I teach now. But in a private school ... I mean, what am I giving them? They have more than everything.

CALLIE. And the Bronx?

SARA. OK. These kids — you know who I was when I was their age? I was the kid who had the right answer, knew I had the right answer but would never raise my hand. Hoping the teacher would call on me anyway. Those are my favorite kids to teach. And here? Now? I've got a classroom full of them. *(Callie looks at the discard pile.)*

CALLIE. Did you pick up a card? *(Sara does.)*

SARA. You should come and meet them one day.

CALLIE. Yeah, OK.

SARA. I'll bet you've never even been to the Bronx.

CALLIE. I go every day.

SARA. *Fly over.*

CALLIE. That's more than most New Yorkers.

SARA. Can I ask you about your job?

CALLIE. *(Dread-filled.)* Go ahead.

SARA. Why the traffic?

CALLIE. Why the traffic indeed.

SARA. I mean, as opposed to news reporting or other kinds of journalism.

CALLIE. I'm not a journalist. I never worked in radio or TV

30

before I got that job.

SARA. So how'd you get it?

CALLIE. My boyfriend Tom's uncle worked at the station.

SARA. Oh.

CALLIE. I mean, it's the traffic it's not even — *the weather.* You just ride around in a helicopter and tell people what the cars are doing.

SARA. The helicopter part is pretty great, right?

CALLIE. Yeah, how great?

SARA. Well if you don't like it you should get another job.

CALLIE. I can't. *(Sara imitates Callie swerving in her imaginary car again. Slight pause.)* I don't get that.

SARA. What time is it? *(Callie looks at her watch.)*

CALLIE. 2:30.

SARA. Already? Is the subway OK this time of night?

CALLIE. You should take a cab.

SARA. How much will that be?

CALLIE. About 10 bucks?

SARA. I'll take the train.

CALLIE. I'll give you the money —

SARA. I have it, it's just too much. It's only four or five stops on the train. *(Callie sits up a little.)*

CALLIE. Listen you can ... you know, you're welcome to stay ... this pulls out to be a sofa bed ... you can take a train in the morning, when it's safe. I'm not getting up for anything in particular.

SARA. Maybe Caesar will come sleep with me.

CALLIE. Yes! You can reconcile with your cat!

SARA. He's holding such a grudge. He never comes out when I'm here.

CALLIE. It took a few days before he started to sleep with me.

SARA. Lucky. *(Slight pause.)*

CALLIE. I'm sure he'll sleep with you tonight.

SARA. Yeah.

CALLIE. Here, let me just get these — *(She pulls off the cushions; Sara helps. Together they pull out the bed.)* I think it's comfortable, I haven't slept on it myself — because I live here, but if it's not comfortable enough then I'll switch beds with you. In

31

fact, should we just do that? You sleep in my room and I'll sleep out here?

SARA. No, no, this'll be fine.

CALLIE. I think it's comfortable. *(Callie bounces on it once, then gets up.)* Is there anything else you need?

SARA. I think I'm all set.

CALLIE. All right. Sleep tight.

SARA. Good night. *(They stand there. Finally, Callie smiles and walks off into her room. Sara takes off her shirt just as Callie reenters with a T-shirt.)*

CALLIE. Do you need a tee — whoop. *(Callie looks away.)*

SARA. It's OK — I have one. *(She pulls one out of her bag.)* We did face painting today so I — *(Callie heads back to the bedroom. Sara puts the shirt on.)*

CALLIE. *(Offstage.)* Good night.

SARA. Sweet dreams. *(Sara gets in bed and shuts out the light. She lies there a minute. Then:)* Psss psssss psss psss psss. *(She lifts her head up and looks for Caesar.)* Caeeeesar. *(No sign of him. Sara lies there another minute.)* Come on you grudge-holder. Pssss psss psss. *(Nothing. Finally, to Callie in the other room.)* Is he in there with you?

CALLIE. Uh-uh. He's not out there with you?

SARA. No. *(Callie walks up to her doorway.)*

CALLIE. Is he under your bed? *(Sara leans over and looks.)*

SARA. No. *(Callie shrugs at Sara.)* Will you do me a favor? For just like a minute?

CALLIE. Sure.

SARA. Would you just lay in bed here for just a minute to see if he comes.

CALLIE. OK.

SARA. Since he's been sleeping with you.

CALLIE. Yeah. *(Callie gets in next to Sara and pulls the covers up.)* I guess we have to convince him we're sleeping.

SARA. Oh, right. *(They lie down.)*

CALLIE. This bed *is* comfortable.

SARA. Isn't it?

CALLIE. I never laid on it before.

SARA. It's comfortable.

CALLIE. I got it second-hand.

SARA. Really?

CALLIE. A hundred and fifty bucks.

SARA. That's cheap.

CALLIE. It's comfortable. *(Pause.)*

SARA. Are your feet hot?

CALLIE. What?

SARA. My feet get hot when I sleep.

CALLIE. Even in winter?

SARA. Yeah.

CALLIE. Take them out.

SARA. I usually move the sheet so that it goes the other way, you know, the short —

CALLIE. OK. *(Sara gets up and turns the sheet around so that both pairs of their feet are exposed. She lies back down. Pause.)*

SARA. Do you see him?

CALLIE. Who?

SARA. Caesar.

CALLIE. Not yet. *(They both lie there staring at the ceiling. After a while:)* Huh? *(Pause.)* Are you asleep? *(No response.)* You're not asleep already, are you? *(She turns to look at Sara who has just shut her eyes. Callie draws her feet under the covers then turns to her side to sleep. Sara opens her eyes.)*

SCENE EIGHT

Callie's apartment. There's loud banging on her door. Callie enters from her bedroom wearing pajamas. She looks through the peephole.

CALLIE. All right George, I hear you! *(She unlocks the door and opens it. George bursts in wearing his bartender uniform.)*

GEORGE. How long have you been home?

CALLIE. Lower your voice.

GEORGE. Why didn't you answer your phone?

CALLIE. I don't know.

GEORGE. You wanna know how fucked up and worried about you everyone is right now?

CALLIE. No.

GEORGE. You wanna know how I heard?

CALLIE. No.

GEORGE. You wanna know exactly what drink I was making at the moment I heard your name on the goddamn TV?

CALLIE. No, I don't.

GEORGE. Dirty martini. TV's on in the background. I hear about this gay bashing, two women attacked and I sort of pay attention, not really. I'm making this drink and thinking about how I gotta run downstairs and get some more peanuts. And then I feel my ears close and my face gets all hot, like I just swallowed a mouthful of hot peppers. So I turn to the TV but now they're talking about some apartment fire. So I switch the channel and they're just starting the story. Gay bashing. Woman in a coma. Callie Pax.

CALLIE. I'm not in a coma.

GEORGE. What?

CALLIE. Sara's in a coma.

GEORGE. How do I know that?

CALLIE. What was I —

GEORGE. How do I know anything but what I see on the goddamn —

CALLIE. What did you want — me to call you from the hospital?

GEORGE. Yes!

CALLIE. What would I say? On a pay phone. In the hospital. Sara lying in a room swollen and blue, face cracked open, knocked out, not responding to anything but the barest reflex — all because ... because —

GEORGE. *Come and get me.* That's what you could've said. *(Pause.)* Are you hurt? *(Callie doesn't respond.)* Did a doctor look at you?

CALLIE. Sara's hurt.

GEORGE. Nothing happened to you? *(Callie doesn't respond. He walks towards her; she walks away.)* Callie —

CALLIE. Bruises.

GEORGE. Where.

CALLIE. Cracked rib.

GEORGE. Let me see.

CALLIE. It's nothing.

GEORGE. Let me see.

CALLIE. There's nothing to see. *(Pause.)*

GEORGE. Do you want me to call anyone?

CALLIE. No *(Slight pause.)*

GEORGE. Do you want me to spend the night?

CALLIE. No.

GEORGE. Do you want me to go? *(Slight pause.)*

CALLIE. No. *(Pause.)* George, do you remember the first time we kissed?

GEORGE. *(Thinks about it.)* No.

CALLIE. Me either. *(Pause.)* You know, I would stand here at the door with Sara and say "good night," "take care," "see ya tomorrow," "get home safe — " When what I *really* wanted to do was plant her a big, fat, wet one. Square on the lips. Nothing confusing about it. She wouldn't have to think, "Maybe Callie meant to kiss me on the cheek and ... missed." You know, just right there. Not between friends. Not a friendly kiss, at all. Bigger. So she'd know. She'd know for sure. That I was answering her. Sara is always asking me "What do you *want, Callie?*" And finally, I let her know. I answered.

SCENE NINE

Callie's apartment. Callie walks in from the kitchen carrying a roasting pan in two mittened hands. She pulls the top off and rears her head back as the smell assaults her. She reaches in and pulls out a drumstick, it's fossilized. She bonks it on the table; it sounds like a baseball bat. There's a knock on the door — Callie starts. She looks out the peephole and sees Sara. She hurries to hide the roasting pan and all signs of cooking. She opens the door and Sara steps in.

SARA. The kids talked about you the rest of the day, you were hilarious.

CALLIE. *(Shady.)* How'd you get in?

SARA. Huh? Oh, there was this woman with a baby carriage. I held the door for her then squeezed in behind her. It smells like something in here.

CALLIE. Like what?

SARA. Like someone vomited in sawdust. Oh — I brought you this — *(She hands her a bottle of wine.)* For coming in and talking to the kids. *(Callie silently takes it and sets it down.)*

CALLIE. It's a little early for me.

SARA. It's ... almost 6:00.

CALLIE. Go ahead, you have some.

SARA. Don't open it for me.

CALLIE. OK.

SARA. *(Trying to figure her out.)* So, what'd you do the rest of the day?

CALLIE. Nothing.

SARA. Nothing?

CALLIE. Nothing.

SARA. You know Michelle, the girl who had the sweater with the puppet on it today? She used to say "nothing" just like that. Until I squeezed an answer out of her.

CALLIE. Those kids adore you.

SARA. Do you think?

CALLIE. You have a knack for them.

SARA. *(As if the first time she's heard it.)* Thank you.

CALLIE. It was humiliating for me.

SARA. Why?

CALLIE. Standing up there talking about my idiotic job.

SARA. You ride in a helicopter, Callie, what could be cooler than that?

CALLIE. Have you noticed? The only thing you ever praise about my job is that I ride in a helicopter? *(Pause.)* But that doesn't even matter. Standing up in front of those kids today telling them about what I do I thought — why should these kids care about traffic, their families don't have cars. *I* don't have a car. No one I care about has a car. Who am I helping?

36

SARA. *(Gently.)* People with cars.

CALLIE. Who are they? Why do they live in New York City? Why have a car when you hear every 10 minutes on the radio that the traffic is so bad?

SARA. Maybe you should look for another job.

CALLIE. Whose uncle's gonna get it for me this time?

SARA. You could get a job based on your experience.

CALLIE. As a traffic reporter?

SARA. What do you want to do instead?

CALLIE. I don't know.

SARA. All right. Come on, we can think about this. What do you like?

CALLIE. I don't want to do this.

SARA. You know a lot about food ... you have great taste in restaurants —

CALLIE. I don't — I really don't want to do this.

SARA. You should become a chef! *(The noise from upstairs starts again. Callie goes for her coat.)*

CALLIE. Let's get the hell out of here.

SARA. You could go to cooking school —

CALLIE. Let's see what's playing at the three-dollar movie theatre.

SARA. You obviously have some kind of talent for food —

CALLIE. Come on, put your coat on, let's go.

SARA. God, what *is* that smell?

CALLIE. I think someone downstairs was trying to cook something.

SARA. Ugh, you think that smell is related to food? *(Callie opens the door for Sara.)*

CALLIE. Barely. *(They exit.)*

SCENE TEN

Sara's hospital room. Callie walks in and stands at the foot of Sara's bed. What can she do? She thinks a beat. She remembers. She untucks the sheet and rolls it back so that Sara's feet are exposed. She looks at Sara — too scared to touch her, then leaves.

SCENE ELEVEN

Callie's apartment. Callie, dressed up, is impatiently waiting for Sara. She paces across the apartment, picking up things, scowling at them, then putting them down. Finally, there's a buzz. She buzzes back and puts on her coat. Sara knocks and Callie opens the door — Sara is holding a wet newspaper over her head.

SARA. Wow, it's really starting to come down now.
CALLIE. That means it's gonna be hard to get a cab.
SARA. We still have time, don't we?
CALLIE. Not really.
SARA. Oh, well, we can be a little late, can't we?
CALLIE. Sara, I asked you to be here by 5:30.
SARA. I know, I'm sorry, I lost track of time. *(Sara takes off her coat.)* Let me just stand next to the radiator for a second.
CALLIE. Is that what you're wearing?
SARA. ... Yeah. *(She looks at her clothes.)* What?
CALLIE. Nothing.
SARA. I mean, is this a dress-up event? *(Callie shrugs.)* What are you wearing?
CALLIE. Just ... clothes.
SARA. Let me see.

CALLIE. It's just ... what I wore to my hippie friend's wedding.
SARA. Let me see? *(Callie opens her coat a little bit.)* Oh. You look great. *(Callie shuts her coat.)* I'm underdressed.
CALLIE. We don't have time to stop by your place.
SARA. Can I borrow something of yours?
CALLIE. Let's just forget it, I don't want to go. *(Callie sits with her coat on.)*
SARA. I thought you had to.
CALLIE. Technically.
SARA. Isn't your station getting an award?
CALLIE. They are, I'm not.
SARA. So do you want to go or not?
CALLIE. I have to.
SARA. OK, let's go. *(Sara makes for the door. Callie remains seated.)* What's going on.
CALLIE. Nothing. *(Pause.)*
SARA. Why are you still sitting down? *(Callie shrugs.)* Let me see what you've got in your closet. *(Sara goes to her bedroom and comes back holding a dress on a hanger.)* Could I wear this?
CALLIE. I wore that to a reception last week.
SARA. You did, I didn't.
CALLIE. People will recognize it.
SARA. Do you care? *(Callie shrugs.)* Callie, what the hell.
CALLIE. I don't know.
SARA. OK. Just tell me. What do you want?
CALLIE. I have to go to this thing.
SARA. Do you not want me to go? Is that it?
CALLIE. You don't have to go if you don't want to.
SARA. Callie, will you say what you want?
CALLIE. I have to go, I have to.
SARA. So let's go. *(She heads for the door.)*
CALLIE. What are you going to wear? *(Sara stops, then turns.)*
SARA. What? *(Callie gets up.)*
CALLIE. I have to go to this thing and I want you to go with me but I don't want you to wear what you're wearing and I don't want you to wear my clothes. What will people think if we walk in together and you're wearing my clothes? *(Sara sits down.)*
SARA. I'm not going.

CALLIE. Now this.

SARA. I'm tired, I'm underdressed, I'm not going to know anyone there except for you — forget it.

CALLIE. Sara, I asked you to go to this thing with me a week ago; I told you it was an awards ceremony, why did you dress like you were going camping?

SARA. You didn't make it sound like it was that big a deal.

CALLIE. An *awards ceremony?*

SARA. If you had wanted me to get dressed up you should've told me.

CALLIE. I told you to be here at 5:30, you couldn't manage that.

SARA. What's the big deal — you don't even like your job.

CALLIE. I don't like my job the way you love your job but that doesn't mean you shouldn't come at the time I asked you to, wearing something appropriate.

SARA. Obviously this is more important than you — *(The clomping from upstairs starts again.)*

CALLIE. There's my cue. I'm leaving now, I don't care what you do.

SARA. Yeah go, get chased out of your own apartment again.

CALLIE. What?

SARA. Better to plan your life around someone else's schedule than have to face them and tell them what you have every right —

CALLIE. What do you care? What do you care? This is my apartment —

SARA. You're pathetic, Callie — *(Callie takes off her coat.)*

CALLIE. Fuck it, I'll stay right here then.

SARA. Perfect.

CALLIE. *You* can leave.

SARA. Glad to.

CALLIE. I'm busy tomorrow so forget about the museum.

SARA. Yeah, I'm busy too. *(Callie opens the door for Sara. Sara grabs her coat and exits. Callie slams the door behind her.)*

SCENE TWELVE

Hospital waiting room. Callie walks in, Peter is already sitting. She recognizes him. Peter looks up, nods politely — as he would to any stranger. Callie sits one seat away from him. Suddenly it occurs to him who she is. After a beat —

CALLIE. Her parents?
PETER. *(Lightly.)* Anita and Joe are in there now, yeah. *(Silence.)*
CALLIE. They're strict about that — the hospital. Two at a time.
PETER. Noah's ark.
CALLIE. Excuse me?
PETER. Two at a — *(He shakes his head at himself.)* — stupid. *(More silence.)*
CALLIE. Did you — was your flight OK?
PETER. There were like six peanuts in the whole — *(He covers his eyes.)* Flight was fine, fine. Thank you.
CALLIE. Her parents, are they — how are they?
PETER. Anita is ... wrecked, *and* Joe — they're ... I mean, Sara's their only daughter —
CALLIE. I know.
PETER. They never wanted her to come here —
CALLIE. I know.
PETER. The doctor said she can't be moved until she regains consciousness.
CALLIE. They want to move her?
PETER. Mm-hm.
CALLIE. Back to St. Louis?
PETER. To Chesterfield, where Anita and Joe live. It's about 20 minutes outside. *(Pause.)*
CALLIE. But what — what if she doesn't want to go?
PETER. Why wouldn't she?
CALLIE. Because the fellowship, she wanted — she worked so hard to get and the kids —

41

PETER. Her old school would take her back in a heartbeat.

CALLIE. Her old school, but she —

PETER. But — I mean we have no idea when she'll be able to go back to work — or *if*. The doctors can't say. There could be permanent ... she'll need rehabilitation, maybe home care —

CALLIE. I know.

PETER. She needs her family. And they need to take care of her. *(Silence.)* ... There was a response.

CALLIE. Excuse me?

PETER. The doctor. He said Sara responded to — he told her to squeeze his hand and she ... squeezed.

CALLIE. She did?

PETER. Yeah.

CALLIE. She did!

PETER. Fucking A.

CALLIE. Amazing!

PETER. I thought you'd want to know. *(Callie looks him in the eye.)*

CALLIE. Thank you. *(Pause.)* Sara ... Sara told me ... nice things ... about you — so many ... *(Pause.)*

PETER. She didn't tell me about you. *(Callie looks down.)* She said you were a friend. *(Pause.)*

CALLIE. I am her friend. *(Pause.)*

PETER. And that you knew good restaurants to go to — *(He looks at Callie.)* That's all Sara told me about you.

CALLIE. I see.

PETER. Sara and I —

CALLIE. She told me. *(Pause.)*

PETER. We lived together for —

CALLIE. Yes. *(Pause.)*

PETER. I still —

CALLIE. Yes. *(Pause.)*

PETER. I'd like — I'd like you to tell me what happened that night. *(Silence. Peter waits long enough to figure out Callie's not going to answer.)* Please. *(Slight pause.)*

CALLIE. I'm sorry.

PETER. What.

CALLIE. I can't.

PETER. Why can't you? *(Slight pause.)*

CALLIE. Everything you need to know has been in the papers, on the TV —
PETER. I've seen the newspapers and the TV.
CALLIE. Then you know every —
PETER. No, I don't know everything. I know what *time* it happened, I know *where* and I know that you were there. And now you're here and *Sara* is in there. That's the part I want to know about. Why is *she* in there.
CALLIE. I wish it was me but it isn't.
PETER. Why isn't it? *(Callie doesn't respond.)* Were *you* hurt?
CALLIE. You don't know what fucking happened.
PETER. Tell me! *(Callie doesn't answer.)* Why couldn't you protect her?
CALLIE. He was big, he was stronger — I tried —
PETER. How big?
CALLIE. I *tried.*
PETER. Bigger than me? *(Callie turns away from him.)* Could I have — *(He turns her back.)* Was he bigger than me?
CALLIE. No! *(Peter steps back. Slight pause.)*
PETER. Why was she protecting you? *(Callie keeps her eyes on his but doesn't answer.)*

SCENE THIRTEEN

Callie's apartment. The phone rings. Her machine picks up. Callie runs in from the bedroom and picks it up.

CALLIE. Hello? *(Dial tone sounds over the speaker. She hangs up. She hovers over the phone for a moment. She jerks the receiver up to her ear, dials a few numbers, then abruptly hangs up. She stares at the phone. She picks up the phone, dials seven numbers, then hangs up. She picks up the phone and places it on the floor in front of the sofa.)* Caesar, please? Come on, you've known her longer than I have. I'll dial her number for you. Tell her I — tell her I thought about —

just tell her to come over. *(Caesar doesn't come out.)* If you were a dog you'd do it. *(Callie picks up the phone and dials seven numbers quickly.)* Hi George, it's me — what. Did you just call here — why not. Yeah, Vong was great. I got the sea bass with cardamom, Sara got the grilled lamb chops with coriander — yeah she eats meat, why wouldn't she? I don't know what you're talking about — Listen, what are you doing for dinner. 'Cause I just walked by Tomoe and noticed there's no line. Come on, I need a sushi fix. All right, if you get there first just tell them — I know you know. OK bye. *(Callie hangs up. She puts the phone back on the floor.)* OK. Caesar, second chance.

SCENE FOURTEEN

Sara's hospital room. Callie walks in and stands at her bedside.

CALLIE. They're finished building that building across from your apartment. *(Sara doesn't respond.)* Wake up now. *(No response. A little stronger.)* Sara. *(No response.)* Can you hear me? *(Callie looks down. Nothing.)* Open your eyes. *(No response.)* Open your eyes. *(No response.)* They're gonna start you on physical therapy tomorrow. Just little stuff, range of motion, something to get your blood moving. *(Pause.)* You've gotten all these cards and letters, I'll read some to you later. *(Pause.)* You know your parents are here. They're doing their best — I think they're doing OK, considering. You getting better makes them feel better — yeah. *(Pause.)* They look at me ... your parents look at me ... like I'm some dirty old man. *(She waits for a response.)* And the newspapers, the TV, the radio — my station, my own station, when they ran the news about the attack, they identified me — "Traffic reporter for this station." Now everybody — the guy at the deli — I used to be the blueberry muffin lady, now I'm the lesbian traffic reporter whose lover got beat up. And I've gotten letters — from two women, their girlfriends were *killed* during attacks — and they wrote me these heartbreaking letters about what they've been through … and they tell me to speak truth to power and I don't know what that *means*, Sara. Do you? Do you know me? *(Callie leans in closer.)* Do you know who I am? *(Sara opens her eyes.)* Oh my God. Hi.

SCENE FIFTEEN

Callie's apartment. Callie walks in from the bedroom in her bare feet wearing a T-shirt and underwear. She pours two glasses of water and drinks from one. George enters from the bedroom wearing jeans and pulling on a T-shirt. Callie hands him the second glass of water. He takes a sip.

GEORGE. Deer Park?
CALLIE. You can't tell.
GEORGE. Tastes like plastic.
CALLIE. You want Evian, you buy it.
GEORGE. Not Evian, *Vermont Natural Springs.*
CALLIE. It's Deer Park or Dos Equis, George. That's what I've got.
GEORGE. Dos Equis, please. *(Callie hands him a beer.)* You got any snacks?
CALLIE. I think I have some wasabi peas.
GEORGE. Those *green* —
CALLIE. Taste like sushi —
GEORGE. Oh *shit.*
CALLIE. What.
GEORGE. I have to go.
CALLIE. Where? *(He goes to get the rest of his clothes.)*
GEORGE. It's someone's birthday at work so a bunch of people are going out to that Japanese tapas place on Ninth Street afterwards, I promised I'd meet them.
CALLIE. Blow them off.
GEORGE. I can't.

CALLIE. Come on. We'll go to Aggie's in the morning for breakfast. Banana pancakes.

GEORGE. I'm sorry, Callie. I made these plans before you called.

CALLIE. Whose birthday?

GEORGE. This new girl at work. I don't think you've met her.

CALLIE. Let me guess. She's an actress. *(He puts on his shoes.)*

GEORGE. She's classically trained.

CALLIE. You gotta get out of the restaurant business, George. Broaden your dating pool.

GEORGE. I'll call — I'll see you on Wednesday, at Jasmine's, right? She's having everyone over for dinner.

CALLIE. Yeah, I put it down. *(He gives her a quick kiss on the lips.)*

GEORGE. Bye. *(He exits and Callie closes the door behind him. She pours his beer down the drain. There's a knock on the door.)*

CALLIE. *(Calling.)* I didn't lock it. *(Sara opens the door halfway and takes a small step in.)*

SARA. I saw your light on — *(Callie turns around, unconsciously pulling on the bottom of her T-shirt.)*

CALLIE. I — I'm not — I didn't know it was you.

SARA. I saw him — just as he was leaving.

CALLIE. Just ... just give me a second. *(Callie pushes the door closed and goes to her bedroom. She comes back out wearing a sweater over her T-shirt and a pair of sweatpants. She opens the door. Sara enters carrying a bottle of wine in a brown wrapper.)*

SARA. I think — I think you'll like this kind. *(Callie takes it and gestures towards the couch. Sara steps tentatively in and sits down on the edge of it.)*

CALLIE. I'll get us some glasses. *(Callie heads for the kitchen.)*

SARA. You don't have to open it now — it's late, I just wanted to — *(Sara gets up and follows Callie.)* Apologize, Callie. You've been so good to me since I came here. I'm embarrassed that I acted, that I said —

CALLIE. That I'm a loser?

SARA. I didn't —

CALLIE. That I'm pathetic.

SARA. You're not pathetic.

CALLIE. I do, I know — I sometimes ... swerve. I was thinking ... you know, when I was little, my parents made me take tennis lessons — I'm not an athlete — neither are my parents, I don't know why — because the lessons were free! And it was summer and my parents didn't want me sitting around the house doing nothing which is what they thought I was doing — which was … true. So, they made me take these lessons, even though I was a klutz, and I tried — but I was a natural klutz. Still, at the end of the summer we all had to play in these tournaments and compete against the kids from the other classes. So for the first round, I get pitted against this kid who obviously took tennis lessons because she wanted to be a really good tennis player. I can't even return her serves. The match takes like 10 minutes. Afterwards, my parents can barely speak, they feel so bad. They take me to Dairy Queen, tell me to order whatever I want — I get the triple banana split and for the rest of the summer they let me sit around and watch *Love Boat* reruns which is all I wanted to do anyway. *(Callie hands Sara a glass of wine.)*

SARA. It was a good show.

CALLIE. But lately, I feel like … there's something … worth … winning.

SARA. Callie, I know that neither you nor I have ever — well at least I know that I haven't, I've never really asked —

CALLIE. By the way, I did get an award.

SARA. What?

CALLIE. An award for traffic reporting — who knew?

SARA. Are you serious?

CALLIE. I'm sorry, I interrupted —

SARA. Did you know?

CALLIE. What.

SARA. You knew you were going to get an award, didn't you?

CALLIE. I swear I didn't.

SARA. Is that why you were so —

CALLIE. Sara, I could never have known. Trust me.

SARA. Did they call you up to the dais and everything?

CALLIE. Just like the Oscars.

SARA. I wish I had seen. *(Sara touches Callie's hand.)*

CALLIE. I wish you'da been there. *(Callie squeezes Sara's hand. Slight pause.)* You want to see it?

SARA. Yes! *(Callie roots through a pile of papers.)*

CALLIE. I thought I stuck it in here. *(Sara goes to the sofa and lifts the pillows.)*
SARA. Sometimes I find stuff in here. *(Sara pulls out a plaque and holds it in the air.)* I found something.
CALLIE. There it is! *(Sara looks at it. She walks over to the bookshelf and slides some photographs out of the way.)*
SARA. Put it here, OK?
CALLIE. Not there.
SARA. Why not?
CALLIE. Everyone will see it.
SARA. Just keep it there. *(Callie reaches for it.)* Stop it. *(Callie takes her hand away but reaches for it again.)* I mean it. *(Callie takes her hand away. Sara takes the plaque, exhales on it, rubs it on her shirt, then puts it back.)*

SCENE SIXTEEN

Sara's hospital room. A nurse is writing on her chart. Callie walks in.

CALLIE. Any good news?
NURSE. She's stable.
CALLIE. I guess that's good news.
NURSE. Her bruises are healing. *(Callie looks at Sara's face.)*
CALLIE. Yes.
NURSE. Can tell she's a pretty girl.
CALLIE. Yeah.
NURSE. She's a schoolteacher?
CALLIE. She is.
NURSE. Where?
CALLIE. In the Bronx. *(Makes eye contact with the nurse.)* Third grade. She has 35 kids. She knew all of their names by the end of the first day.
NURSE. Takes a lot to be a public school teacher in New York City.

CALLIE. She's got it.

NURSE. Those kids are lucky.

CALLIE. They know it.

NURSE. I'm gonna give her her bath now.

CALLIE. Oh, all right. *(She starts to leave.)*

NURSE. I'll show you so you can do it. *(Callie stops. Slight pause.)*

CALLIE. Oh — that's very — but I don't think I should, I've never —

NURSE. You've seen the worst of her. Most of her bruises are on her face. Her body looks fine. If that's what you're afraid of.

CALLIE. I don't know if she'd want me to.

NURSE. It won't hurt my feelings, you know. I'm sure she'd like it better if you do it.

CALLIE. ... Right now, though, I have to go. *(She taps on her watch face.)* The time. But ... thank you. *(She heads out.)*

SCENE SEVENTEEN

Callie's apartment. Callie and Sara walk in. Sara carries groceries, Callie carries a bag from a record store.

CALLIE. Which airport is he flying into?

SARA. JFK.

CALLIE. At 11:00?

SARA. 11:30.

CALLIE. Have the car service pick you up at around 10:30, tell them to take the BQE to the LIE to the Van Wyck — that'll get you to the airport by 11:00. But tell the driver to take the Midtown Tunnel back, it'll cost you three-fifty but the Manhattan-bound traffic on the Williamsburg bridge will be too heavy.

SARA. Check. *(Sara looks through the CDs.)* Do you ever go out dancing?

CALLIE. Sometimes I do — my friend Sheila goes to this club on Wednesday nights and sometimes she invites a bunch of us girls to go.

SARA. I'd like to go sometime.

CALLIE. ... Sure ...

SARA. Will you let me know next time you go?

CALLIE. A bunch of us girl friends go ... it's fun ... the music's great and it's fun, you don't have to worry about guys trying to pick you up ... 'cause it's all women. I like to go there and dance, there's this kind of warm — like when you go to the bathroom, there's only one line and everyone's really nice and smiles ...

SARA. Have you ever ... asked someone to dance?

CALLIE. We kind of stick to each other — us friends. Sheila usually knows a bunch of women there and I've met them.

SARA. You ever meet a woman there, that seemed ... interesting ... to you?

CALLIE. ... No. *(Slight pause.)* Not there. *(Pause.)* Have you — ?

SARA. What.

CALLIE. In St. Louis, do they — or have you been to?

SARA. We have a couple places like that but I've never been. My friend Janet says that only college girls go to the clubs and bars; older lesbians just stay home and read. That's what everyone in St. Louis does, stays home and brews their own beer or does their e-mail. *(Slight pause.)*

CALLIE. But I mean, have you ever...?

SARA. I mean I can't imagine any woman who's never felt attracted —

CALLIE. Right!

SARA. It's just, I mean if you've never actually *been* —

CALLIE. You want a beer?

SARA. Love one.

CALLIE. I hope I have some.

SARA. What time is it?

CALLIE. Just about 6:00.

SARA. Uh-oh.

CALLIE. What?

SARA. I promised my roommates I'd clean the apartment by the time they came back from their trip and they're gonna be home in an hour.

CALLIE. Just — wait here a couple more minutes.

SARA. I really should go.

CALLIE. Just wait one minute.

SARA. Why?

CALLIE. I wanna ... show you something.

SARA. Callie —

CALLIE. Take my watch. *(Callie takes off her watch and hands it to Sara.)* What time is it now?

SARA. 5:59.

CALLIE. And how many seconds?

SARA. 38 seconds.

CALLIE. And what day is today?

SARA. Thursday.

CALLIE. What time is it now?

SARA. 5:59 and 50 seconds.

CALLIE. So count 'em.

SARA. What?

CALLIE. Count 'em down. Five seconds, four —

SARA. Four, three, two, one — what. *(Callie opens her hands towards Sara.)* What? *(Callie gestures towards the ceiling.)* It's quiet. Oh! *(Callie nods.)* It's Thursday at 6:00! And it's quiet! *(Callie points her thumbs towards herself. Sara opens her arms and they hold each other. They keep holding — Callie lets go.)* I'll call you tomorrow.

CALLIE. OK. *(Pause.)*

SARA. Um, see ya.

CALLIE. OK. Bye. *(Sara opens the door and lets herself out. Callie ambles slowly over to the sofa, looks at the door, buries her head in a pillow and screams.)*

SCENE EIGHTEEN

A coffee shop. Mrs. Winsley is sitting at a table. Callie walks in.

CALLIE. Mrs. Winsley?

MRS. WINSLEY. Yes. *(Callie extends her hand; Mrs. Winsley*

shakes it.)
CALLIE. I'm sorry I'm late. I came straight —
MRS. WINSLEY. It's fine, it's fine. I don't have to meet my husband until 8:00. *(She gestures for Callie to sit.)*
MRS. WINSLEY. Should we order something? Coffee or tea?
CALLIE. Coffee would be great.
MRS. WINSLEY. How are you doing?
CALLIE. I'm OK.
MRS. WINSLEY. Yeah?
CALLIE. I want to thank you for … what you did, Mrs. Winsley.
MRS. WINSLEY. I only did what I should've.
CALLIE. Not everybody —
MRS. WINSLEY. How's your girlfriend?
CALLIE. Sara — she's better. Alert and responding. We just have to wait to see what kind of effect. How much and what.
MRS. WINSLEY. I read in the paper she's from Kansas or something?
CALLIE. St. Louis. Missouri. Kansas City is in Missouri but Sara's from St. Louis.
MRS. WINSLEY. I'm from outside Cincinatti myself, although I've been here 20 years. When I first moved here I would smile at strangers on the subway, give quarters to beggars on the street.
CALLIE. Sara gives a dollar.
MRS. WINSLEY. So I can imagine what it must've seemed like to her. Small-town girl in the big city — seeing men dressed as women, women holding hands — must've seemed like gay paradise to her.
CALLIE. St. Louis is not a small town.
MRS. WINSLEY. She's at St. Vincent's, isn't she?
CALLIE. Yes.
MRS. WINSLEY. How are the doctors there? Are you pleased with them?
CALLIE. It's hard to say. You want them to do everything, you want them to make her better. But they do what they can, I think they're OK.
MRS. WINSLEY. How do you find it — spending all your time there. I mean I know they have limited visiting hours but they probably let you stay all day.
CALLIE. I have to go to my job —

MRS. WINSLEY. Of course. I didn't mean to imply —
CALLIE. But I do visit every day.
MRS. WINSLEY. It must be exhausting for you.
CALLIE. Well, her family's here —
MRS. WINSLEY. Are you close with them?
CALLIE. No ... Not close.
MRS. WINSLEY. I know what it's like with in-laws. It took years before mine ... Have you and Sara been together long?
CALLIE. Um ... no.
MRS. WINSLEY. Oh, I'm sorry I thought you two were —
CALLIE. I know.
MRS. WINSLEY. Here I've been talking as if —
CALLIE. It's OK.
MRS. WINSLEY. So you're not really —
CALLIE. No, like I said I go there every —
MRS. WINSLEY. But you're not really involved.

SCENE NINETEEN

Callie's apartment. George, wearing jeans and a dress shirt, checks himself out in the full-length mirror. Callie walks in from the bedroom wearing a dress.

GEORGE. I'm a little strapped 'cause business was slow last night.
CALLIE. Just don't worry about it.
GEORGE. I brought 50 bucks.
CALLIE. That'll get you a salad.
GEORGE. How expensive is this place?
CALLIE. Expensive.
GEORGE. Why do we have to go to a place like that? Why can't we just go to Benny's Burritos and drink a bunch of margaritas.
CALLIE. I *told* you, I'm gonna pay for the whole thing so stop stressing out about it. *(She pushes George out of the way with her hip and looks at herself in the mirror.)*

GEORGE. OK. Miss Traffic Reporter of the Universe or whatever you are, I'm gonna get the lobster.

CALLIE. They have venison.

GEORGE. *(Even better.)* Ooo! *(Callie turns towards him.)*

CALLIE. Does this dress make me look fat? *(He looks away.)*

GEORGE. I *can* not, *will* not, *ever* answer that question.

CALLIE. I'm changing. *(She heads for the bedroom.)*

GEORGE. What are you so uptight about?

CALLIE. *(Offstage.)* I'm not uptight.

GEORGE. That's the third time you've changed. Who is this guy anyway?

CALLIE. *(Offstage.)* Sara's ex.

GEORGE. Why do you need to look so good for him? *(Callie comes back on wearing a different dress. She stands in front of the mirror.)*

CALLIE. It's a nice restaurant.

GEORGE. Is he gonna be dressed up? You told me I could wear jeans.

CALLIE. Because I knew you'd wear jeans anyway.

GEORGE. *(Has to admit she's right.)* Hm. *(George stands next to Callie; he looks at their reflection. He puts his arm around her waist.)*

CALLIE. So how was the birthday party the other night? *(She wriggles away.)*

GEORGE. Fine.

CALLIE. Did the birthday girl get everything she asked for?

GEORGE. You want to talk about this?

CALLIE. No.

GEORGE. Cool. *(Pause.)*

CALLIE. Did you fuck her before or after midnight?

GEORGE. Nice.

CALLIE. I'm just wondering about the technicality —

GEORGE. Listen, I'm not like you and that guy —

CALLIE. Who.

GEORGE. Who was that, that guy with the nose ring that you —

CALLIE. Hey —

GEORGE. In the bathroom of the —

CALLIE. Hey —

GEORGE. With no protection. *(The buzzer buzzes.)*

CALLIE. I told you *that?*

GEORGE. I asked.

CALLIE. We should start keeping more to ourselves.

GEORGE. Too late.

CALLIE. Don't say that.

GEORGE. Why not? *(There's a knock on the door.)*

CALLIE. Makes me feel old.

GEORGE. We are old.

CALLIE. You are. *(Callie opens the door. Sara walks in alone, also wearing a dress. Callie looks behind her.)*

CALLIE. ... Hi.

GEORGE. Hey, how's it going.

SARA. *(Small.)* Hi.

CALLIE. Where's Peter?

SARA. He ... uh, left. You look beautiful. So do you, George.

CALLIE. He left ... New York?

SARA. Yeah, he changed his flight. He left a couple hours ago. I told him to tell the driver to take the Van Wyck.

CALLIE. Something happen at work?

SARA. No it — I asked him to leave. *(Callie moves closer to her.)*

CALLIE. Oh, um — *(She looks at George, then back at Sara.)* Listen, we don't have to go out —

GEORGE. Yeah, no, if you're upset —

SARA. No, it's fine, I want to go out. I want to get to know George.

CALLIE. Are you — did something happen — *(Again she looks at George.)* I mean, you don't have to — *(George stands behind Callie and puts his hands on her shoulders. She looks at his hands — what are they doing there?)*

SARA. He was being so — he was criticizing everything. "Your apartment's too small. It's in a bad neighborhood. Your school is dangerous. It's too far away." All he could talk about was how dirty and dangerous everything is.

CALLIE. ... Well —

GEORGE. It *is.*

SARA. What? Compared to St. Louis? I don't want to live there. I've started something here and I — that's what — because it's ... I love ... New York!

GEORGE. *(Nods.)* Mm.

CALLIE. Let's go eat.

GEORGE. *(To Sara.)* Are you sure?

SARA. Yeah.

GEORGE. Great! Let's go! *(George offers Sara his arm. She takes it. He offers his other arm to Callie.)*

CALLIE. I'll catch up with you.

GEORGE. OK. *(To Sara, on the way out.)* They have venison you know.

SARA. You mean Bambi? *(George and Sara exit. Callie walks over to the Magic Eight-Ball, shuts her eyes a moment, then wiggles the ball. She looks at its answer.)*

CALLIE. *(Quietly.)* Yes! *(She puts down the ball and hurries to catch up with them.)*

SCENE TWENTY

Sara's hospital room. She's sitting in a wheelchair, eyes open. She's visibly weak on her right side. Peter sits next to her reading from a book.

PETER. "And then 98 kilometers — that's 61 miles — north of Wilcannia is a lunar landscape." That looks lunar, doesn't it? "Some of the locals don't mind showing off the interiors of their white-walled subterranean settlements" — You'll want to sign up early for *that* tour, heh heh — *(He looks at Sara, clears his throat, then goes back to the book.)* As I was saying, "Looping around about 160 kilometers — that's 100 miles to you and me — a road leads to Mootwingee, a surprising patch of greenness in the barren Bynguano — " Australia *is* an English-speaking country, isn't it? *(He fingers the last few chapters of the book.)* You know, I'm just dying to see how this ends but can we — *(Sara nods. He kisses her hand.)* Thank you. We'll save the big finish for after dinner. *(He puts the book away and picks something up.)* Did you see this? *(He holds a homemade greeting card in front of her. Callie steps into the room, then steps back. She watches.)* You got a card from your old class at Friends. See, there's Matthew and Sophia and Emily — your favorite, the anti-Christ. She writes, "I hope you feel bitter and come bark soon." I see your replacement is letting her spelling skills slip. *(Sara tentatively takes the card in her hand.)* Hey! Look at you.

I've been talking to Jenny and Steve a lot, keeping them updated. Jenny's been letting everyone know what's going on. Margaret's called, Jamie, Lisa — it's frustrating for them not to be able to see you. They picture the worst, all they have are the images in their heads from reading the newspaper articles. It'll be better for them when they can see you.

The doctor says we can move you soon. Your parents and I have been talking. I agree that you should stay with them after you get out of rehab. You're *welcome* to stay at our old place, of course, if you want to, I would take off from work so that I could — I'm going to take off from work anyway. *(Pause.)* Just because you're coming back home I'm not going to act like everything is going to be the way it was. I know you went to New York because you wanted to change things. *(He touches her face.)* You do want to go home — *(Water drops from Sara's eyes.)* Don't you? *(Callie turns, walks towards Sara's nurse, who is standing at her station.)*

CALLIE. Excuse me.

NURSE. You're back.

CALLIE. Do you have time now?

NURSE. Yeah.

CALLIE. To show me how to do it?

SCENE TWENTY-ONE

Callie's apartment. Callie and Sara enter after leaving the restaurant. Callie takes off her coat; Sara doesn't.

CALLIE. Uugggh, I'm so full I can't stand up. What do you want to do, we could watch a movie if you want —

SARA. Let's uh ... let's go out, let's go somewhere.

CALLIE. Where do you want to go?

SARA. There's a bar. In the West Village. Henrietta's, you ever been?

CALLIE. Once.

SARA. Will you go with me?

CALLIE. *(She looks at her dress.)* Like this?

SARA. We could change. Friday night, it's supposed to be a good night.

CALLIE. OK. *(Slight pause.)* Good for what?

SARA. There's supposed to be a lot of people there.

CALLIE. *(Nods though she doesn't quite understand.)* OK, let's go.

SARA. You change, and then we can stop by my place and then we'll go.

CALLIE. We don't — you can borrow some of my clothes.

SARA. That's better. That's great. *(They stand there.)* You go ahead and change and I'll ... change next. I'll wear whatever's left over.

CALLIE. I'll go change.

SARA. Maybe we'll like it there — *(She looks helplessly at Callie.)*

CALLIE. *(Trying to be helpful.)* Yeah, OK.

SARA. Let's just —

CALLIE. We'll go, we'll hang out, have a drink.

SARA. Yes! You know, maybe meet people.

CALLIE. Are you — I mean, do you ... want to *meet* people?

SARA. Yes! — No! I want to meet people to — meet people maybe make friends but no, I don't want to meet *someone*, some stranger —

CALLIE. We'll just go.

SARA. It's just a bar.

CALLIE. With a whole bunch of lesbians in it.

SARA. And us. *(They lock eyes, hoping the other will say something perfect. They keep waiting.)*

SCENE TWENTY-TWO

The hospital. Sara's sitting in a wheelchair. Callie enters carrying a bag.

CALLIE. Sara. *(Sara turns to her.)* I brought you stuff to change into. *(She pulls some clothes out of the bag.)* Don't you think? *(Callie puts them in Sara's lap.)* We're gonna do this. Watch me. You gotta listen to me too. *(She undoes Sara's gown.)* OK, we're gonna start with the left side because we're taking things off. *(She takes off Sara's left sleeve.)* And now the right. *(She helps Sara pull her arm out of the right sleeve. She takes out a bra.)* This closes in front. Can you ... go like this? *(She lifts her arms at the elbows. Sara does it.)* Good for you. I should tell — *(She looks around for the nurse.)* Later. *(She puts the bra on.)* So far so good. *(She takes the shirt off Sara's lap.)* Nice shirt, huh? Did I pick out a nice shirt for you? OK, you're gonna need to sit up a little for me. *(Sara sits up. Callie guides Sara's weak right arm through the sleeve. It's difficult.)* If I can just — am I hurting you? I'm sorry, Sara, I'm sorry. *(To herself.)* Relax. *(She puts the left sleeve on.)* This one you can do. Push — push — *(It gets caught.)* Keep breathing, and push — *(Sara pushes her arm through the sleeve.)* It's a girl! *(Callie buttons Sara's shirt.)* Let's keep you warm. It's cold in this place. *(Callie takes the pants. She helps Sara's right foot off the footrest.)* We're gonna do this together. I'll do this one. *(She then points to her left.)* That one you can do. *(Sara takes her left leg off; it spasms.)* Oh — oh. OK. OK. *(Callie flips the foot pads up. She scrunches up the right leg of the pants and wrangles it on.)* We gotta work together on this one, OK? *(She scrunches up the left leg. Sara lifts her leg.)* Are you helping me? Yes. You are. The shoes go last. *(Callie puts her right shoe on.)* Like this. *(Sara slips her left foot in the left shoe.)* And like that. *(She pushes Sara's feet closer to her. Callie stands up.)* Now you're gonna stand up. I'm gonna help. One, two, three — *(She puts her hands under Sara's arms and lifts her up. She pulls her pants up. Sara loses her balance; Callie tries to ease her down; they both come down with a thud.)* I can do this, you see? *(Sara nods.)* Choose me. *(Sara smiles.)*

SCENE TWENTY-THREE

Sara and Callie are walking down the street, having just left Henrietta's. Finally, Sara turns to Callie.

SARA. *What* was I thinking.
CALLIE. That was like — going to a birthday party when you don't know the person whose birthday it is.
SARA. I don't know why I was expecting ... I don't know what I was expecting. What time is it? *(Callie checks her watch.)*
CALLIE. Around 4:00.
SARA. So late.
CALLIE. Should we ... go somewhere — where do you want to go?
SARA. I don't know —
CALLIE. Let's just ... keep walking.
SARA. Sure. *(They walk a few steps in silence. After a while.)*
CALLIE. How do you eat corn on the cob. Around the world or typewriter-style?
SARA. *Typewriter.*
CALLIE. Me too.
SARA. What kind of person eats around the world?
CALLIE. I don't know.
SARA. I mean, what is that based on? You read left to right, right?
CALLIE. I do.
SARA. So you should eat your corn that way too.
CALLIE. Do you think in Egypt they eat right to left?
SARA. I don't know.
CALLIE. Fascinating question, though.
SARA. Do you wait *in* line or *on* line.
CALLIE. Oh. Now I wait on line. But I used to wait in.

SARA. But physically, you're *in* a line, not *on* one, right?

CALLIE. Yeah, stick by your guns. I caved in.

SARA. You say on. I say in.

CALLIE. What about this? *(Callie plants her one. They pull away.)*

SARA. Huh.

CALLIE. What?

SARA. You just did that.

CALLIE. Yes I did.

SARA. Nice. *(They come at each other but with their heads angled towards the same side. They bump noses.)*

CALLIE. Whoop —

SARA. Sorry — *(They back away. Callie puts her arms around Sara's waist and pulls her towards her.)*

SARA. Do you think we should —

CALLIE. I don't want to go anywhere, I don't want to change anything. Let's just —

SARA. OK.

CALLIE. Try again. *(They get their heads right, connect lips, put their arms around each other. And kiss.)*

End of Play

PROPERTY LIST

Bottle of wine
Coats/Jackets
Drinking glasses

CDs (CALLIE, SARA)
CD player (CALLIE)
Black tape (CALLIE)
Phone (CALLIE)
Watches (CALLIE, GEORGE)
Newspaper (CALLIE)
Dirty socks (CALLIE)
Box of Kleenex (CALLIE)
Mail (CALLIE)
Videotapes (CALLIE)
Bra (CALLIE)
Pet carrier (SARA)
Pile of books (SARA)
Large key ring (SARA)
Candlestick (SARA)
Two coffee mugs (CALLIE)
Magic Eight-Ball (CALLIE)
Report (DET. COLE)
Bottles of beer (CALLIE)
Menu (CALLIE)
Bouquet of flowers (CALLIE)
Vase (CALLIE)
Several hangers of clothes (CALLIE)
Remote control (GEORGE)
Bouquet of baby roses (SARA)
Giant playing cards (SARA)
T-shirts (CALLIE, SARA, GEORGE)
Bags (SARA, CALLIE)
Roasting pan (CALLIE)
Oven mitts (CALLIE)
Drumstick (CALLIE)
Wet newspaper (SARA)

Dress on hanger (SARA)
Bottle of water (CALLIE)
Shoes (GEORGE)
Pile of papers (CALLIE)
Plaque (SARA)
Photographs (SARA)
Chart (NURSE)
Groceries (SARA)
Bag from record store (CALLIE)
Book (GEORGE)
Homemade greeting card (GEORGE)
Clothes for Sara (bra, shirt, pants, shoes) (CALLIE)

SOUND EFFECTS

'70s disco song
Phone ringing
Door buzzer
George's voice on answering machine
Loud and rhythmic clomping on ceiling
Callie's answering machine
Dial tone

NEW PLAYS

★ **MOTHERS AND SONS by Terrence McNally.** At turns funny and powerful, MOTHERS AND SONS portrays a woman who pays an unexpected visit to the New York apartment of her late son's partner, who is now married to another man and has a young son. Challenged to face how society has changed around her, generations collide as she revisits the past and begins to see the life her son might have led. "A resonant elegy for a ravaged generation." –NY Times. "A moving reflection on a changed America." –Chicago Tribune. [2M, 1W, 1 boy] ISBN: 978-0-8222-3183-7

★ **THE HEIR APPARENT by David Ives, adapted from Le Légataire Universel by Jean-François Regnard.** Paris, 1708. Eraste, a worthy though penniless young man, is in love with the fair Isabelle, but her forbidding mother, Madame Argante, will only let the two marry if Eraste can show he will inherit the estate of his rich but miserly Uncle Geronte. Unfortunately, old Geronte has also fallen for the fair Isabelle, and plans to marry her this very day and leave her everything in his will—separating the two young lovers forever. Eraste's wily servant Crispin jumps in, getting a couple of meddling relatives disinherited by impersonating them (one, a brash American, the other a French female country cousin)—only to have the old man kick off before his will is made! In a brilliant stroke, Crispin then impersonates the old man, dictating a will favorable to his master (and Crispin himself, of course)—only to find that rich Uncle Geronte isn't dead at all and is more than ever ready to marry Isabelle! The multiple strands of the plot are unraveled to great comic effect in the streaming rhyming couplets of French classical comedy, and everyone lives happily, and richly, ever after. [4M, 3W] ISBN: 978-0-8222-2808-0

★ **HANDLE WITH CARE by Jason Odell Williams.** Circumstances both hilarious and tragic bring together a young Israeli woman, who has little command of English, and a young American man, who has little command of romance. Is their inevitable love an accident…or is it destiny, generations in the making? "A hilarious and heartwarming romantic comedy." –NY Times. "Hilariously funny! Utterly charming, fearlessly adorable and a tiny bit magical." –Naples News. [2M, 2W] ISBN: 978-0-8222-3138-7

★ **LAST GAS by John Cariani.** Nat Paradis is a Red Sox-loving part-time dad who manages Paradis' Last Convenient Store, the last convenient place to get gas—or anything—before the Canadian border to the north and the North Maine Woods to the west. When an old flame returns to town, Nat gets a chance to rekindle a romance he gave up on years ago. But sparks fly as he's forced to choose between new love and old. "Peppered with poignant characters [and] sharp writing." –Portland Phoenix. "Very funny and surprisingly thought-provoking." –Portland Press Herald. [4M, 3W] ISBN: 978-0-8222-3232-2

DRAMATISTS PLAY SERVICE, INC.
440 Park Avenue South, New York, NY 10016 212-683-8960 Fax 212-213-1539
postmaster@dramatists.com www.dramatists.com

NEW PLAYS

★ **ACT ONE by James Lapine.** Growing up in an impoverished Bronx family and forced to drop out of school at age thirteen, Moss Hart dreamed of joining the glamorous world of the theater. Hart's famous memoir *Act One* plots his unlikely collaboration with the legendary playwright George S. Kaufman and his arrival on Broadway. Tony Award-winning writer and director James Lapine has adapted Act One for the stage, creating a funny, heartbreaking and suspenseful celebration of a playwright and his work. "...brims contagiously with the ineffable, irrational and irrefutable passion for that endangered religion called the Theater." –NY Times. "...wrought with abundant skill and empathy." –Time Out. [8M, 4W] ISBN: 978-0-8222-3217-9

★ **THE VEIL by Conor McPherson.** May 1822, rural Ireland. The defrocked Reverend Berkeley arrives at the crumbling former glory of Mount Prospect House to accompany a young woman to England. Seventeen-year-old Hannah is to be married off to a marquis in order to resolve the debts of her mother's estate. However, compelled by the strange voices that haunt his beautiful young charge and a fascination with the psychic current that pervades the house, Berkeley proposes a séance, the consequences of which are catastrophic. "...an effective mixture of dark comedy and suspense." –Telegraph (London). "A cracking fireside tale of haunting and decay." –Times (London). [3M, 5W] ISBN: 978-0-8222-3313-8

★ **AN OCTOROON by Branden Jacobs-Jenkins. Winner of the 2014 OBIE Award for Best New American Play.** Judge Peyton is dead and his plantation Terrebonne is in financial ruins. Peyton's handsome nephew George arrives as heir apparent and quickly falls in love with Zoe, a beautiful octoroon. But the evil overseer M'Closky has other plans—for both Terrebonne and Zoe. In 1859, a famous Irishman wrote this play about slavery in America. Now an American tries to write his own. "AN OCTOROON invites us to laugh loudly and easily at how naïve the old stereotypes now seem, until nothing seems funny at all." –NY Times [10M, 5W] ISBN: 978-0-8222-3226-1

★ **IVANOV translated and adapted by Curt Columbus.** In this fascinating early work by Anton Chekhov, we see the union of humor and pathos that would become his trademark. A restless man, Nicholai Ivanov struggles to dig himself out of debt and out of provincial boredom. When the local doctor, Lvov, informs Ivanov that his wife Anna is dying and accuses him of worsening her condition with his foul moods, Ivanov is sent into a downward spiral of depression and ennui. He soon finds himself drawn to a beautiful young woman, Sasha, full of hope and energy. Finding himself stuck between a romantic young mistress and his ailing wife, Ivanov falls deeper into crisis, heading toward inevitable tragedy. [8M, 8W] ISBN: 978-0-8222-3155-4

DRAMATISTS PLAY SERVICE, INC.
440 Park Avenue South, New York, NY 10016 212-683-8960 Fax 212-213-1539
postmaster@dramatists.com www.dramatists.com

NEW PLAYS

★ **I'LL EAT YOU LAST: A CHAT WITH SUE MENGERS by John Logan.** For more than 20 years, Sue Mengers' clients were the biggest names in show business: Barbra Streisand, Faye Dunaway, Burt Reynolds, Ali MacGraw, Gene Hackman, Cher, Candice Bergen, Ryan O'Neal, Nick Nolte, Mike Nichols, Gore Vidal, Bob Fosse…If her clients were the talk of the town, she was the town, and her dinner parties were the envy of Hollywood. Now, you're invited into her glamorous Beverly Hills home for an evening of dish, dirty secrets and all the inside showbiz details only Sue can tell you. "A delectable soufflé of a solo show…thanks to the buoyant, witty writing of Mr. Logan" –NY Times. "80 irresistible minutes of primo tinseltown dish from a certified master chef." –Hollywood Reporter. [1W] ISBN: 978-0-8222-3079-3

★ **PUNK ROCK by Simon Stephens.** In a private school outside of Manchester, England, a group of highly-articulate seventeen-year-olds flirt and posture their way through the day while preparing for their A-Level mock exams. With hormones raging and minimal adult supervision, the students must prepare for their future — and survive the savagery of high school. Inspired by playwright Simon Stephens' own experiences as a teacher, PUNK ROCK is an honest and unnerving chronicle of contemporary adolescence. "[A] tender, ferocious and frightning play." –NY Times. "[A] muscular little play that starts out funny and ferocious then reveals its compassion by degrees." –Hollywood Reporter. [5M, 3W] ISBN: 978-0-8222-3288-9

★ **THE COUNTRY HOUSE by Donald Margulies.** A brood of famous and longing-to-be-famous creative artists have gathered at their summer home during the Williamstown Theatre Festival. When the weekend takes an unexpected turn, everyone is forced to improvise, inciting a series of simmering jealousies, romantic outbursts, and passionate soul-searching. Both witty and compelling, THE COUNTRY HOUSE provides a piercing look at a family of performers coming to terms with the roles they play in each other's lives. "A valentine to the artists of the stage." –NY Times. "Remarkably candid and funny." –Variety. [3M, 3W] ISBN: 978-0-8222-3274-2

★ **OUR LADY OF KIBEHO by Katori Hall.** Based on real events, OUR LADY OF KIBEHO is an exploration of faith, doubt, and the power and consequences of both. In 1981, a village girl in Rwanda claims to see the Virgin Mary. Ostracized by her schoolmates and labeled disturbed, everyone refuses to believe, until impossible happenings appear again and again. Skepticism gives way to fear, and then to belief, causing upheaval in the school community and beyond. "Transfixing." –NY Times. "Hall's passionate play renews belief in what theater can do." –Time Out [7M, 8W, 1 boy] ISBN: 978-0-8222-3301-5

DRAMATISTS PLAY SERVICE, INC.
440 Park Avenue South, New York, NY 10016 212-683-8960 Fax 212-213-1539
postmaster@dramatists.com www.dramatists.com

NEW PLAYS

★ **AGES OF THE MOON by Sam Shepard.** Byron and Ames are old friends, reunited by mutual desperation. Over bourbon on ice, they sit, reflect and bicker until fifty years of love, friendship and rivalry are put to the test at the barrel of a gun. "A poignant and honest continuation of themes that have always been present in the work of one of this country's most important dramatists, here reconsidered in the light and shadow of time passed." –NY Times. "Finely wrought…as enjoyable and enlightening as a night spent stargazing." –Talkin' Broadway. [2M] ISBN: 978-0-8222-2462-4

★ **ALL THE WAY by Robert Schenkkan. Winner of the 2014 Tony Award for Best Play.** November, 1963. An assassin's bullet catapults Lyndon Baines Johnson into the presidency. A Shakespearean figure of towering ambition and appetite, this charismatic, conflicted Texan hurls himself into the passage of the Civil Rights Act—a tinderbox issue emblematic of a divided America—even as he campaigns for re-election in his own right, and the recognition he so desperately wants. In Pulitzer Prize and Tony Award–winning Robert Schenkkan's vivid dramatization of LBJ's first year in office, means versus ends plays out on the precipice of modern America. ALL THE WAY is a searing, enthralling exploration of the morality of power. It's not personal, it's just politics. "…action-packed, thoroughly gripping… jaw-dropping political drama." –Variety. "A theatrical coup…nonstop action. The suspense of a first-class thriller." –NY1. [17M, 3W] ISBN: 978-0-8222-3181-3

★ **CHOIR BOY by Tarell Alvin McCraney.** The Charles R. Drew Prep School for Boys is dedicated to the creation of strong, ethical black men. Pharus wants nothing more than to take his rightful place as leader of the school's legendary gospel choir. Can he find his way inside the hallowed halls of this institution if he sings in his own key? "[An] affecting and honest portrait…of a gay youth tentatively beginning to find the courage to let the truth about himself become known." –NY Times. "In his stirring and stylishly told drama, Tarell Alvin McCraney cannily explores race and sexuality and the graces and gravity of history." –NY Daily News. [7M] ISBN: 978-0-8222-3116-5

★ **THE ELECTRIC BABY by Stefanie Zadravec.** When Helen causes a car accident that kills a young man, a group of fractured souls cross paths and connect around a mysterious dying baby who glows like the moon. Folk tales and folklore weave throughout this magical story of sad endings, strange beginnings and the unlikely people that get you from one place to the next. "The imperceptible magic that pervades human existence and the power of myth to assuage sorrow are invoked by the playwright as she entwines the lives of strangers in THE ELECTRIC BABY, a touching drama." –NY Times. "As dazzling as the dialogue is dreamful." –Pittsburgh City Paper. [3M, 3W] ISBN: 978-0-8222-3011-3

DRAMATISTS PLAY SERVICE, INC.
440 Park Avenue South, New York, NY 10016 212-683-8960 Fax 212-213-1539
postmaster@dramatists.com www.dramatists.com